Aggie Football Legends

By Anthony Andro
Original cover art by Mark Hoffer

Great Texas Line Press
Fort Worth, Texas

Aggie Football Legends

For bulk sales
and whole inquiries
contact:
Great Texas Line Press
Post Office Box 11105
Fort Worth, TX 76110
greattexas@hotmail.com
www.greattexasline.com

*To see our complete list of Texas guide, humor and cook
books, visit: www.greattexasline.com*

Editor: Tom Johanningmeier
Cover: Mark Hoffer
Copy Editor: Bernie Diemer
Proof Editor: Amy Culbertson

**Great Texas Line Press strives to be socially responsible, donating a
portion of proceeds from several books to Habitat for Humanity of Fort
Worth, North Fort Worth Historical Society, Texas Dance Hall Preservation
Inc. and Terlingua's Big Bend Educational Foundation. Hundreds of books
are donated annually to public-radio stations throughout Texas for fund-
raising. Every effort is made to engage Texas writers, editors, illustrators,
designers and photographers who fell victim to the newspaper industry
crisis, and to produce the books at local, family-run print shops.**

Contents

A circa 1900 football practice.

Introduction

There are football teams that have won more games and more national championships than Texas A&M.

But few, if any, can match the Aggies for the intangibles the football program brings with its traditions, loyal fans and game-day environment.

Those who don't understand what happens in Aggieland like to say it's more like a cult than a school. Again, those are the ones who don't understand.

Since that first game in 1894 — a humiliating 38-0 loss to the University of Texas — the Aggies have been building a football team big on winning and tradition.

In the 119 years that have followed, there have been national championships, Heisman Trophies, memorable seasons, forgettable seasons and plenty in between. There have been Buckys and Bubbas and Dats and Vons. A John David every now and then has also been good for the cause.

The years and players have come and gone but the Aggie fight exemplified in that first game has never wavered. The 12th Man is stronger than ever. And the football program is squarely in the nation's spotlight, thanks to Heisman Trophy winner Johnny Manziel and the school's move to the Southeastern Conference.

How do you capture 119 years in a little book? With an open mind, for sure. All Aggies may bleed maroon, but they know it hasn't always been as good as it is now.

Anthony Andro

Texas A&M's squad that played its first game in 1894.

Cushng Memorial Library and Archives,
Texas A&M University

And so it begins

Fittingly, Texas A&M's football program began in 1894 with a game against Texas. But it was all Longhorns in a 38-0 victory. The Aggies managed to finish .500 when they beat Galveston Ball High School 14-6. (In those days rivals included high schools). Two years later, they posted their first undefeated season, going 2-0-1 with wins against Austin College and Houston High School.

Perfection

Fans might question the Aggies' claims of 1919 and 1927 championships, but there's no denying the 1939 squad, which finished 11-0 and beat fifth-ranked Tulane, 14-13, in the Sugar Bowl to claim the national championship.

How good were they? They outscored opponents 212-31, recorded six shutouts and allowed only eight points in Southwest Conference games. TCU (six points) and SMU (two) were the only conference teams to score against A&M.

Running back John Kimbrough and offensive tackle Joe Boyd were All-Americans. Kimbrough finished fifth in the Heisman Trophy voting and, along with halfback Jim Thomason, was a first-round draft pick. Kimbrough was drafted by the Chicago Cardinals; Thomason went to the Detroit Lions. Kimbrough rushed for 159 yards against Tulane and finished with more than 1,300 in his career.

Talk about defense

The 1939 national championship team was known for its suffocating defense. But it was nothing compared to the effort Dana X. Bible's squad put up in 1919.

That team didn't allow a point in outscoring its opponents 275-0.

Bible coached the Aggies in 1917 but missed the 1918 season because of World War I. That team went 6-1 under D.V. Graves, with the loss a 7-0 setback to Texas.

A&M started its 1919 season with a double-header (yes, there were double-headers in those days), beating Sam Houston State 77-0 and San Marcos 28-0. The Aggies squeaked out 7-0 victories against Southwestern and Texas down the stretch.

The team featured three future members of the Texas A&M Hall of Fame: guard W.E. Murrah, multi-athlete Roswell Higginbotham and fullback Jack Mahan, who threw the javelin in the 1920 Antwerp Olympics. Higginbotham played some semi-pro baseball and ended up coaching the A&M baseball team.

There was no Associated Press championship at the time, but decades later, mathematician Richard Billingsley's computer rankings and the National Championship Foundation were wise enough to tab the Aggies national champs.

The Junction Boys

For younger Aggies, there are two ways to learn about the Junction Boys: Watch the awful made-for-TV movie in which Tom Berenger plays Paul "Bear" Bryant or read Jim Dent's account of the Aggies' late-summer trip to Junction in 1954.

Bryant's stunt wouldn't work today. Too much media. Too many lawyers.

It was his first season at A&M, and Bryant thought that many players were weak and had been poorly coached. Wanting to get away from the distractions of College Station for training camp, he took the team to Junction, which was suffering through a drought and brutal heat wave.

The fields were littered. The players slept in metal huts that became too hot to touch in the searing heat. And water breaks? Forget it. Water is for the weak. Practices started before sunrise and lasted all day.

The camp was supposed to last two weeks, but so many players were dropping out that Bryant cut it to 10 days.

At one point, a reporter from Houston showed up after hearing about dissension, according to a *Sports Illustrated* article.

"Now, son, are you gonna quote me on this?" Bryant asked the reporter.

"Yes, sir."

"Well, you can call your boss and tell him I said if there isn't any dissension now, there's damn sure going to be some in a hurry, and I'm going to cause it."

Among the 27 camp survivors were Jack Pardee, Gene Stallings and Dennis Goerhing.

Their suffering resulted in *one* win the next season.

But they followed that miserable season by going 7-2-1 in 1955 and 9-0-1 in '56 for their first Southwest Conference championship since 1941.

Seven players from that 1956 team were named all-conference. Three were Junction survivors.

<blockquote>
" "We'd taken the team down to Junction to find out right off who the players were and who the quitters were, and the quitters had outnumbered the players three to one." "

Paul "Bear" Bryant, as quoted by *Sports Illustrated* in 1966
</blockquote>

At a Junction reunion in 1979, Bryant was given a ring inscribed with the words *Junction Boys*. When Bryant died four years later, he was wearing that ring. It was the only piece of jewelry he wore, even though he led Alabama to six national championships.

Poor T-sips

Forget that Texas holds a 76-37-5 series edge against the Aggies.

Let's focus on what really matters: the Aggies' dominance from 1984-94, when A&M won 10 of 11 games. And the only loss — a 28-27 setback on Dec. 1, 1990 — was tainted by CBS commentators who announced what play the Aggies were going to run as they went for the victory with a two-point conversion attempt.

Even the Longhorns can stop a play when they know what's coming.

The Aggies outscored the Longhorns 318-146 over the 11 games, and half of their 10 wins were by at least two touchdowns.

About that title game ...

The top-ranked Kansas State Wildcats were all set to play for the 1998 national championship. All they had to do to was beat the lowly Aggies in the Big 12 championship game. A&M had won the South Division but was coming off a loss to Texas.

But the Aggies overcame a 15-point fourth-quarter deficit on touchdown passes by Brandon Stewart to force overtime. The teams traded field goals in the first OT. Then Stewart found Sirr Parker, who tiptoed into the end zone for the game-winning score.

Who cares that Parker appeared to have been knocked out of bounds? The win sent the Aggies to the Sugar Bowl, where they were thumped 24-14 by Ohio State.

Parker's magic gave the Aggies their only Big 12 title in football.

As for K-State's national title plans? The Wildcats fell to the Alamo Bowl, where they lost to Purdue, 37-34.

The bonfire game

The game against Texas went on as scheduled in 1999, in front of 86,128 grieving fans at Kyle Field. They were mourning the loss of 12 people who were killed when a four-story pyramid of logs collapsed as they were preparing for the annual bonfire, which symbolized the school's burning desire to beat Texas.

Now, eight days later, the 24th-ranked Aggies were facing No. 5 Texas, which had already clinched the Big 12's South Division title. Trailing 16-6 at halftime, the Aggies stormed back after an emotional halftime during which the Texas band played *Amazing Grace* and raised the flags of Texas A&M.

"It was a weird time, you know? You're getting ready to play a football game, and the team on the other side is actually being nice," Aggies wide receiver Greg Porter told the Bryan *Eagle*.

Running back Ja'Mar Toombs started the comeback by scoring his second touchdown of the game on a 9-yard run with 4:47 remaining in the third quarter. The Aggies took the lead late in the fourth when Randy McCown found Matt Bumgarner in the right corner of the end zone for a 14-yard score with 5:02 remaining.

Texas had two more chances but couldn't get the ball across midfield. With less than a minute remaining, the Aggies' Jay Brooks forced a fumble by Texas quarterback Major Applewhite, and linebacker Brian Gamble pounced on the loose ball to seal the victory for R.C. Slocum's team.

In a lasting image, Gamble fell to his knees and raised his hands to the sky.

> A lot of guys felt like they couldn't practice, knowing there were still people lying under that pile of wood. It was like it was our brothers, because we're a part of the A&M family.

Linebacker Roylin Bradley,
as quoted by the Bryan *Eagle*

Score one for Chet

You won't find Chet Brooks on Texas A&M's list of letter-winners. That's because he's listed under *Terrance*. While he made an impact as a defensive back from 1984-87, the biggest mark he left is being felt today.

He's the guy who named the Aggies' stingy defense the "Wrecking Crew." It's been used ever since, even though some porous units during the 2000s probably made Brooks and his teammates wince.

But the early squads lived up to the name: The Aggies' defense was ranked in the Top 10 six times from 1985-95, and only twice did teams average more than 300 yards per game against the Aggies. The 1991 team registered a record 56 sacks and led the nation in total defense, allowing just 222.4 yards per game.

Better than the truth

Making fun of the University of Texas should be a sport in College Station, although it's too easy and everyone would win.

But the legend behind the name of the Longhorns' mascot is a lot better than the truth. The story goes that Texas named the longhorn steer "Bevo" in an attempt to save face after some Aggies branded the animal "13-0," the score of the Aggies' big win in 1915. So Texas rebranded the steer, making a *B* out of the *13* and squeezing an *EV* in front of the *0.*

Great story. Too bad it's not true.

The Aggies did brand the steer, but he got his name when the editor of the Texas Exes magazine, the *Alcalde*, in describing a game referred to the mascot as "Bevo," according to an account in the UT History Central website.

AGGIE FACT

The score of the Aggies' big win in 1915 was burned into the hide of Texas' mascot.

It must have been good eating for the Aggies in 1920. That's when the original Bevo — which years earlier had been branded 13-0 by Aggies after a big win — was barbecued for the Texas football banquet because the school didn't have enough money to take care of him. The Aggies were invited by their rivals. They were served the side they branded and got to keep the hide. Any story that ends with free barbecue can't be all bad.

Bucky ball

He wasn't a particularly good passer. Couldn't really run, either. But no one symbolizes the success of the Aggies in the mid-1980s as much as quarterback Bucky Richardson.

In 1987, Richardson, then a freshman, came off the bench and led the Aggies to a 27-14 victory over Southern Miss and its quarterback, Brett Favre. He was named the Southwest Conference Newcomer of the Year and rushed for 98 yards and two touchdowns in the Aggies' 35-10 win over Notre Dame in the Cotton Bowl. Then, in his senior season of 1991, he led the Aggies to the Southwest Conference title, passing for more than 1,400 yards and rushing for 448. Twice he accounted for more than 340 yards of total offense.

AGGIE NUMBER

31 Aggies on NFL rosters as of June 2012.

John Football I

Long before there was Johnny Football, there was another John, who also happened to win a Heisman Trophy: running back John David Crow, who won the award in 1957.

Crow rushed for 562 yards, scored six touchdowns, threw five TD passes and recorded five interceptions in only seven games as the Aggies finished 8-3 under coach Bear Bryant. He was inducted into the College Football Hall of Fame in 1976. After a professional career with the Chicago Cardinals, Crow returned to Texas A&M as an assistant athletic director in 1983. He was the school's athletic director from 1988-93.

1957 Heisman voting

1.	RB John David Crow	Texas A&M
2.	DL Alex Karras	Iowa
3.	RB Walt Kowalczyk	Mich. State
4.	OL Lou Michaels	Kentucky
5.	QB Tom Forrestal	Navy
6.	E Jimmy Phillips	Auburn
7.	RB Bob Anderson	Army
8.	OL Dan Currie	Mich. State
9.	RB Clendon Thomas	Oklahoma
10.	QB Lee Grosscup	Utah

The rise and fall of Johnny Football

I t's hard to remember but Johnny Manziel was once the talk of college football for all the right reasons. Back in 2012 Manziel became the first freshman to win the Heisman Trophy.

It started in the second game of the season when Manziel threw for 294 yards, ran for another 124 and accounted for three touchdowns in a 49-3 win over the SMU Mustangs.

2012 Heisman voting

1. QB Johnny Manziel	Texas A&M
2. LB Manti Te'O	Notre Dame
3. QB Collin Klein	Kansas State
4. WR Marqise Lee	USC
5. QB Braxton Miller	Ohio State
6. DL Jadeveon Clowney	S. Carolina
7. QB Jordan Lynch	Northern Ill.
8. WR Tavon Austin	W. Virginia
9. RB Kenjon Barner	Oregon
10. LB Jarvis Jones	Georgia

Receiver Uzoma Nwachukwu referred to Manziel as "Captain Amazing." Then center Patrick

Lewis said: "You've got to keep blocking because he'll make plays when there are no plays to be made. I guess that's why they named him 'Johnny Football.'"

The nickname stuck and it led to a magical season. It also included a file to protect the moniker with the U.S. Patent and Trademark Office.

An autograph-signing scandal clouded his sophomore season and, despite passing for more yards and touchdowns, there was no Heisman repeat. He was selected in the first round of the NFL Draft by the Cleveland Browns. But in typical Cleveland fashion, he was a bust. That turned out to be the least of his problems. He was dogged by substance-abuse concerns and charged with misdemeanor domestic violence after an incident with his girlfriend at the time (the charges were later dropped). He was out of the NFL after just two seasons and seven touchdown passes.

Manziel cleaned up his act in 2017 in a comeback bid. He played in the Spring League in Austin and signed with the CFL's Hamilton Tiger-Cats in May 2018. The CFL probably won't lead to a return to glory for Manziel, but he'll always have 2012.

Heisman moment

E very Heisman Trophy winner has a signature game or play that propels him into the Heisman picture.

Johnny Manziel had both during A&M's stunning 29-24 victory over then-No. 1 Alabama on Nov. 10, 2012.

AGGIE FACT The first win in 10 tries vs. No. 1 teams came on Nov. 9, 2002, against Oklahoma. Freshman quarterback Reggie McNeal came off the bench to throw four touchdown passes, and Terrance Kiel's interception in the final minutes sealed a 30-26 victory. It was an improbable victory: The Aggies entered the game 5-4 after two consecutive losses and didn't win another after knocking off the Sooners.

A&M was a two-touchdown underdog, but Manziel and the Aggies bolted to a 20-0 first-quarter lead. Manziel's second touchdown might have sealed the Heisman.

In the stats, it was a 10-yard touchdown pass to Ryan Swope. On the field, it was another instance of Manziel turning disaster into a big play. The pocket quickly collapsed after Manziel took the snap on third-and-goal. Facing a rushing defender, Manziel stepped forward and banged into one of his blockers.

The collision knocked the ball from Manziel's hand, but he managed to gather it in, spin, reverse direction and fire a touchdown pass to Swope in the back of the end zone.

"This is one of those meaningful experiences where, when you reflect back on your college career, you say, 'We did something great,' " A&M defensive end Damontre Moore told reporters after the game.

Manziel accounted for more than 350 yards and led the Aggies to just their second victory over a No. 1-ranked team. He joined Oklahoma's Charles Thompson (1987) as the only freshmen quarterbacks to beat a No. 1 team on the road.

The stunning performance put Manziel in the national spotlight. It never left him.

Heisman hunters

H as anyone seen Tim Brown's precious towel — the one that led to an unsportsmanlike penalty for him in the 1988 Cotton Bowl? He could have used it to wipe his tears after the Aggies kept him in check.

Brown, the Heisman Trophy winner, got flagged when he tried to tackle 12th Man Warren Barhorst, who had ripped the towel from Brown on a kickoff and trotted to the Aggies sideline with it. Brown finished with six catches for 105 yards and a touchdown, but his Notre Dame Fighting Irish were blown out, 35-10.

Defensive back Chet Brooks came up with the idea to swipe Brown's towel, according to *Texas A & M: Where Have You Gone?* by Rusty Burson. Brooks and Brown, both from Dallas, had played against each other in high school, and Brooks knew it would drive Brown crazy if someone yanked his towel off, Burson wrote.

AGGIE FACT There have been numerous All-Americans and two Heisman Trophy winners at Texas A&M. But only one player holds the honor of being the first Aggie to appear on the cover of *Sports Illustrated*. That goes to Bubba Bean, who appeared on the Dec. 8, 1975, issue under the headline, "Texas A&M stakes its claim." No. 44 is seen running by a Texas defender. Bean ran for **944** yards in '75 in leading the Aggies to a

Cushing Memorial Library and Archives, Texas A&M University

Bubba Bean appeared on a *Sports Illustrated* cover.

share of the Southwest Conference title. He left A&M as the school's all-time leading rusher. (His **2,846** yards now ranks seventh at A&M).

"Those guys had been stealing our towels all day, and I swiped it and started running off the field while trying to stuff the towel in my pants," Barhorst said in Burson's book.

"I was pretty shocked when Brown jumped on my back. I guess he got the towel back. I have always assumed the towel fell out and Brown picked it up."

Brown wasn't the only Heisman Trophy winner to be handled by the Aggies. Auburn's Bo Jackson (1985 winner) and BYU's Ty Detmer (1990) were also bowl-game losers against Texas A&M.

After scoring on a 73-yard pass reception, Jackson didn't do much as A&M thumped the Auburn Tigers, 36-16, in the 1986 Cotton Bowl.

And poor Detmer couldn't even match Brown's and Jackson's limited success when he faced the Aggies in the 1990 Holiday Bowl.

Detmer and his BYU Cougars teammates thought they deserved better than a Holiday Bowl matchup against the lowly Aggies. Detmer left with a 65-14 whipping and a pair of separated shoulders.

Detmer might have been the Heisman winner, but he wasn't the best quarterback on the field. That honor went to Bucky Richardson, named the Most Valuable Player after throwing for a touchdown, running for two and catching a touchdown pass.

As for Detmer? He threw for 120 yards and was knocked out of the game in the third quarter.

Either that, or he was looking for Brown's towel to cry in.

'The Hit'

True Aggie fans remember "The Hit," even after more than 20 years.

Today, the hit would have gotten All-American linebacker Quentin Coryatt ejected. In 1991, it was named ESPN's Hit of the Year.

It happened when TCU receiver Kyle McPherson cut across the middle and stretched his arms to get a hand on a pass. At that instant, Coryatt barreled into the defenseless player, driving his helmet into the receiver's chin.

AGGIE NUMBER

$450,000,000

Cost of the 2013-15 renovations
to Kyle Field.

> **My intentions were not to hurt him. I played the game at a very intense level, and that was the outcome of it.**
> **It's a part of the game.**

Quentin Coryatt, as quoted by the *Houston Chronicle* on his 1991 hit on a player that was recognized by ESPN

McPherson fell to the ground and lay motionless for a moment. His broken jaw was wired shut for two months. He doesn't remember the play.

The grainy video has registered more than 4.5 million views online. Unfortunately for Coryatt, "The Hit" was his career highlight. He was a first-round selection of the Indianapols Colts but never amounted to much in seven seasons.

Pencil in 100

Before he was an NFL bust and long before he was in legal trouble, Darren Lewis was a force in the Aggie backfield. His breakout season was in 1988, when he ran for 168 yards against Oklahoma State in the third week. He reeled off 10 consecutive 100-yard games that season and finished with 128 against Alabama.

Lewis and 100-yard games were common at A&M. His first came against Southern Mississippi in 1987, and his last came in the Holiday Bowl rout of BYU in 1990. In that game Lewis needed just five carries to rush for 104 yards. In his four-year career, Lewis set a school record with 27 100-yard games and five 200-yard games.

He finished second in the nation in rushing in 1988 and third in 1990.

Not surprisingly, Lewis is the all-time leading rusher in school history with 5,012 yards.

In January 2013, he was charged in the robbery of a Duncanville 7-Eleven.

The 12th Man

The Seattle Seahawks have tried to claim their stadium is home to the "Twelfth Man," but as any maroon-and-white-loving Aggie can tell you, there's only one 12th Man.

The tradition began in 1922 when Dana X. Bible's Aggies were shorthanded against Centre College. E. King Gill, who was not in uniform, was called from the stands. He suited up and stood ready to play. He never got in the game, but the Aggies won, 22-14.

Gill's gesture came to represent the feeling of all students in Aggieland. That's why they stand during games and wave "12th Man" towels. That's why the slogan *Home of the 12th Man* lines the wall at Kyle Field. A statue of Gill stands outside the stadium's north entrance.

Jackie Sherrill started the 12th Man Team when he used non-scholarship players on the kick-off squad and ended up with the nation's

AGGIE FACT The Aggies shocked the college football world in 1982 by hiring Jackie Sherrill away from Pitt with an annual salary of $267,000, by far the highest salary for a football coach at the time. (His base salary at Pitt was $66,000.)

A 2,300-word *Sports Illustrated* article reported concern the Aggies may have gone "financially berserk."

"I'm afraid this will start an escalation in the bidding I don't like to see," former Michigan athletic director Don Canham told the magazine. "Suddenly money doesn't mean anything. It becomes plastic. Everything is all out of whack."

Said Lou Holtz, who was coaching at Arkansas at the time: "This money tells people all over the country how important the people at Texas A&M think football is."

Adjusted for inflation, Sherrill's salary equates to $699,000 in 2012.

So have the Aggies gone "financially beserk"? Coach Kevin Sumlin's 2013 salary? $3.1 million.

best kick coverage. Under R.C. Slocum the tradition changed, and one player wore No. 12, representing the student body. Other coaches have used variations of the 12th Man.

Reveille I was given a formal military funeral on the football field in 1944.

Watchful eyes

In her afterlife, Reveille — the dog that is the school's mascot and highest-ranking member of the Corps of Cadets — keeps watch over the Aggies from her eternal resting place outside the north end of Kyle Field.

The tradition began in 1944, when Reveille I was given a formal military funeral on the football

The kidnapping of Tech Beauty is just one of many pranks involving the Aggies and an animal. In 1963, Texas Tech's mascot, a 9-year-old quarter horse, went missing before its game against Texas A&M. Tech students combed the rural areas in hopes of finding the mare, according to the *Lubbock Avalanche Journal*. A backup horse filled in for the game, and Tech Beauty was found the next day, tied to a trough in a barn near Idalou. Tech Beauty had been shaved and the letters AMC were painted on its side.

field. Since then, the mascots have been buried in the cemetery, which has a view of the scoreboard.

How die-hard is Reveille in her afterlife? When renovations made it impossible for the Reveilles to see the scoreboard from six-feet under, a small scoreboard was added outside the stadium.

That's dedication to the Aggie cause.

Who needs cheerleaders?

There's absolutely nothing wrong with the cheerleaders in the SEC. There wasn't anything wrong with the ones in the Southwest Conference of the Big 12 either.

But the Aggies don't need girls to get the fans fired up. That's the job of the Yell Leaders, who lead the 12th Man in yells known as Farmers Fight, Beat the Hell and Horse Laugh, to name just a few.

AGGIE FACT A note in their seats reminds the media: The press box sways. More than 80,000 strong, fans rock back and forth as the *Aggie War Hymn* is played, causing the press box to move.

Since 1907, the Aggies have used Yell Leaders to fire up fans at football games. Using hand signals to signify the yell, Yell Leaders lead the Aggie fans during football games. Yell Leaders are five students who are elected by the student body, and since 1931 their football work week has begun with Midnight Yell, where every Aggie knows practice makes perfect.

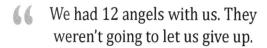

We had 12 angels with us. They weren't going to let us give up.

Quarterback Randy McCown after the bonfire game, as quoted by *The Dallas Morning News*

Free ride?

In the early 1980s, the Aggies thought they had Sealy running back Eric Dickerson, who had committed to Texas A&M. After all, the story goes, "someone" gave him a Pontiac Trans Am to help get him to College Station. But on Signing Day, Dickerson jilted the Aggies and signed with SMU. Suddenly, he wasn't driving the car.

At SMU, Dickerson and Craig James teamed to become the Pony Express, leading the Ponies to the top of the nation's rankings. But soon the NCAA shut down the SMU program because the boosters couldn't stop themselves from paying the players.

In February 2013, Dickerson broke his silence and told the *Houston Chronicle* that the Trans Am story was a "total myth." He said he got the car from his grandmother, who raised him. But was it destroyed by Aggies' fans? Nope. Dickerson told the paper that the car was stolen after he sold it to a friend.

So that explains it ...

Maybe there was a reason Texas A&M was so good in the 1980s and early 1990s. At least the NCAA saw it that way. The Aggies were penalized twice for recruiting violations and boosters' payments to players.

It began in 1985, when an assistant parked a Datsun 280ZX in front of a recruit's house and told him that the sports car could be his

AGGIE NUMBER

.337

The worst winning percentage for a decade by A&M. During the 1960s, the Aggies won just 31 games.

if he signed with the Aggies. Another recruit was told that his dad's medical bills would be taken care of. Then there was the player who was paid $4,150 for work at a booster's warehouse, even though he didn't work all of the hours. And of the hours he did work, he got $15 an hour, which, ad-

> **" It is apparent that some alumni
> and student-athletes still believe
> they can violate NCAA rules
> with impunity. "**

NCAA infractions report in 1994, after the Aggies became
one of only three universities to receive seven public
penalties for rules violations

justed for inflation would be $34 in 2012. There were also $100 checks for "gas money" and "Christmas shopping."

In September 1988, the NCAA hit the Aggies with a two-year postseason ban and scholarship cuts.

"I'm responsible," said Jackie Sherrill, the Aggies' coach and athletic director, who quit with one game remaining in the 1988 season. "It's my job. I'm responsible for the program and to make sure things are done correctly."

Just six years later, the Aggies were at it again.

One booster paid nine players more than $27,000 to work at his apartment complex. The NCAA said the players were usually paid $400 every two weeks regardless of the amount of work they did, and that meant they were overpaid $17,920. Among the players caught up in that investigation: standout running back Greg Hill, who pocketed nearly $18,000, according to The Associated Press.

The Aggies were placed on five years' probation, banned from appearing on TV and playing in a bowl in 1994.

That's probably why the Aggies turn up on those online lists of the country's dirtiest college programs.

> " The state of Texas, football and rules violations go together like ham, egg and cheese. Might deserve a higher slot, but the Aggies' cheat-to-win ratio is low. In other words, it hasn't been money well spent. "
>
> Mike Freeman of CBS SportsLine.com,
> on football's dirtiest programs

How many titles?

Before moving to the SEC, the Aggies tried to spruce up their résumé by adding a few more titles to Kyle Field's championship wall, which had honored the undisputed 1939 team. But then workers added "1919" and "1927," and the Aggies became the butt of jokes nationwide.

Various outfits ranked Harvard and Illinois as national champions in 1919. The Aggies are basing their claim on the National Championship Foundation, which was formed in 1980 and voted on past champions. It awarded four titles in 1993

1957

The last year the Aggies were ranked No. 1 nationally. That team started the season 8-0 before losing the final three games.

.798 The best winning percentage for a decade by A&M. During the 1910s, the Aggies went 67-14-3.

and five in 1991. The 1927 championship is based on a system established in 1935.

The Aggies aren't the only ones to claim retroactive titles. Others are rewriting history based on new votes or formulas.

The Aggies also claimed Big 12 titles in 1997 and 2010. In 1997, Nebraska beat the Aggies 54-15 in the Big 12 championship game. In 2010, the Aggies tied for the South Division with Oklahoma and Oklahoma State, but lost the tiebreaker. Officials say they are going to add the word *South* below those years.

'Bold step' changed A&M and SWC

In 1965, A&M football coach Gene Stallings spoke out against integration, saying the Aggies weren't ready for it.

Ten years later, led by a recruiting class that included nine black players, the Aggies rolled to one of their best seasons in school history, reaching No. 2 in the rankings and sharing the 1975 Southwest Conference Championship.

Cushing Memorial Library and Archives, Texas A&M University

Jerry Honore: A&M's first black recruit.

Ever since, African-Americans have been among the stars of Aggie football.

The culture change came from Emory Bellard, who replaced Stallings in 1972, and who was the first coach in the SWC to recruit black players in large numbers. They led the Aggies to 10-2 records in 1975 and 1976.

A&M had been all-white until 1963. Four years later, Samuel Williams and James Reynolds walked on, becoming the team's first black players. Jerry Honore was the team's first black recruit, signed by Stallings in 1971, according to Richard Pennington, author of *Breaking the Ice: Racial Integration of Southwest Conference Football*.

"Not many people appreciate what a bold step that was, to bring in nine black players to a place that had virtually no blacks," former A&M coach R.C. Slocum told the *Houston Chronicle* in February 2011 after Bellard died at 83. Slocum was a defensive assistant for Bellard.

Dean Campbell, another Bellard assistant, told the Arkansas fan website Hawgs Illustrated: "The thing he changed in the Southwest Conference was the way the black athlete was recruited. At that time, teams were signing one or two black athletes per class. We were signing 10 or 12 at A&M. Emory told us to go get the best players. More than anyone else, he changed the color of the teams in the league."

The battle between Texas A&M and Baylor was known as the Battle of the Brazos.

Riot on the Brazos

Texas A&M and Baylor enjoyed a spirited rivalry known as the Battle of the Brazos, but in 1926 it was marred by the death of a cadet during a halftime brawl.

As a Baylor homecoming float neared the section where the Corps of Cadets were sitting, a cadet ran from the stands and tried to steer the vehicle from the corps. The women fell off the truck, and chairs, sticks and fists started flying.

"The Aggies had problems with Baylor the year before, when Baylor was making fun of the A&M yells," former Baylor archivist Tommy Turner Sr. told the *Houston Chronicle* in 1990. "They thought the Model A or T was bucking, appearing to make fun of the A&M yells again."

The melee ended after the Aggie band began playing *The Star Spangled Banner,* causing the cadets to snap to attention, according to an account by Bartee Haile, who writes a syndicated newspaper column on Texas history.

Lt. Charles Milo Sessums, a senior cadet from Dallas, took a blow to the head and died the next morning at a Waco hospital.

Within the week, Haile wrote in his column, a committee of Aggies released a public statement: "We apologize to the ladies of Baylor for this incident, because one of our traditions is that no A. and M. man has ever willingly or knowingly harmed a woman."

Athletic events between the schools were suspended for four years.

Other hijinks weren't as serious, according to accounts on Baylor News Online and an 1990

> " The 1956 Baylor game, without a question, was the toughest football game I ever remember playing in. I remember it vividly. Things went on in pileups that I would not want to discuss in a family newspaper. I guess the Baptists don't like Aggies, or maybe the Aggies don't like Baptists. "

1957 Heisman Trophy winner John David Crow, as quoted by the *Houston Chronicle* in 1990

article in the *Houston Chronicle*: In 1936, Aggies added red stripes to a flagpole and posted a sign on Waco Hall predicting the score: "A and M 50, Baylor 0." (They tied 0-0).

In 1950, Aggies planted oats in the grass of Baylor Stadium, which was under construction. The sprouts read "A and M."

In the 1950s, two Aggies stole Baylor's young mascot and were driving back to College Station when he got scared and started tearing up the car. Twenty miles outside of Waco, they set the bear free. Reports didn't say what happened to the cub.

48

5 legendary teams

1939: First to win AP title

Of course you've got to have the only Aggie team to win the Associated Press national title on the list. A&M beat fifth-ranked Tulane in the Sugar Bowl. Six of the 11 wins were shutouts.

Sept. 23	at Oklahoma State	W, 32-0
Sept. 30	Centenary (La.)	W, 14-0
Oct. 7	at Santa Clara	W, 7-3
Oct. 14	Villanova	W, 33-7
Oct. 21	at TCU	W, 20-6
Oct. 28	Baylor	W, 20-0
Nov. 4	at Arkansas	W, 27-0
Nov. 11	SMU	W, 6-2
Nov. 18	at Rice	W, 19-0
Nov. 30	Texas	W, 20-0
Jan. 1	at Tulane	W, 14-13

1919: Ten shutouts

This team won a national title, but the remarkable thing was the defense, which didn't allow a point all season. The Aggies outscored their opponents

Sept. 27	Sam Houston St.	W, 77-0
Oct. 4	Texas State	W, 28-0
Oct. 11	at SMU	W, 16-0
Oct. 18	Howard Payne	W, 12-0
Oct. 25	Trinity (Texas)	W, 42-0
Nov. 1	Oklahoma State	W, 28-0
Nov. 8	TCU	W, 48-0
Nov. 15	at Baylor	W, 10-0
Nov. 22	Southwestern (Texas)	W, 7-0
Nov. 27	Texas	W, 7-0

275-0. All but two of the wins came by double figures.

An Aggie team from the 1910s, Texas A&M's winningest decade.

1994: Tie only blemish

Ineligible for a bowl berth, the Aggies were 10-0-1, with the tie a surprising 21-21 outcome against SMU. Seven wins came by at least two touchdowns for a team that ended the season ranked eighth.

Sept. 3	at LSU	W, 18-13
Sept. 10	Oklahoma	W, 36-14
Sept. 24	Southern Miss	W, 41-17
Oct. 1	Texas Tech	W, 23-17
Oct. 8	at Houston	W, 38-7
Oct. 15	Baylor	W, 41-21
Oct. 22	Rice	W, 7-0
Oct. 29	SMU	T, 21-21
Nov. 5	at Texas	W, 34-10
Nov. 12	at Louisville	W, 26-10
Nov. 19	TCU	W, 34-17

1992: Perfect until bowl

R.C. Slocum's Aggies started this season with Jeff Granger, who went on to be a first-round pick in baseball, as their quarterback. They were 12-0 heading into the Cotton Bowl, where the No. 5 Notre Dame trounced the No. 4 Aggies, 28-3.

Aug. 26	Stanford	W, 10-7
Sept. 5	at LSU	W, 31-22
Sept. 12	Tulsa	W, 19-9
Sept. 19	at Missouri	W, 26-13
Oct. 3	Texas Tech	W, 19-17
Oct. 17	Rice	W, 35-9
Oct. 24	Baylor	W, 19-13
Oct. 31	at SMU	W, 41-7
Nov. 7	Louisville	W, 40-18
Nov. 12	at Houston	W, 38-30
Nov. 21	TCU	W, 37-10
Nov. 26	at Texas	W, 34-13
Jan. 1	Notre Dame	L, 28-3

1975: Decade's best

The best Aggie team of the 1970s started the season ranked ninth and rolled to a 10-0 record and No. 2 national ranking after beating Texas 20-10. But the Aggies' bid for a national title was derailed when Arkansas thumped them, 31-6, the last game of the season. Instead of playing for a national title, the Aggies went to to the Liberty Bowl, where they lost to USC 20-0.

Sept. 13	Mississippi	W, 7-0
Sept. 20	at LSU	W, 39-8
Sept. 27	Illinois	W, 43-13
Oct. 4	at Kansas State	W, 10-0
Oct. 11	at Texas Tech	W, 38-9
Oct. 18	at TCU	W, 14-6
Oct. 25	Baylor	W, 19-10
Nov. 8	SMU	W, 36-3
Nov. 15	at Rice	W, 33-14
Nov. 28	Texas	W, 20-10
Dec. 6	at Arkansas	L, 31-6
Dec. 22	USC	L, 20-0

5 legendary coaches

Jackie Sherrill

(1982-88, 52-28-1)

Sherrill replaced Tom Wilson following the 1981 season. The Aggies were 16-16-1 in Sherrill's first three seasons, but he got things turned around in 1985, leading the Aggies to a 10-2 record and their first Southwest Conference title since they were tri-champs a

Year	Record	SWC record	Final ranking
1982	5-6	3-5	
1983	5-5-1	4-3-1	
1984	6-5	3-5	
1985	10-2	7-1	6
1986	9-3	7-1	12
1987	10-2	6-1	9
1988	7-5	6-1	

decade earlier. Sherrill's Aggies won three SWC titles and beat Texas the last five times his teams faced the Longhorns. His conference winning percentage of .676 ranks just behind R.C. Slocum's.

Paul "Bear" Bryant

(1954-57, 25-14-2)

There were some dark days in College Station before Bryant took over in 1954. The Aggies had just two winning seasons in the previous eight years and won only four games from 1947-49. At first, it didn't

Year	Record	SWC record	Final ranking
1954	1-9	0-6	
1955	7-2-1	4-1-1	14
1956	9-0-1	6-0	5
1957	8-3	4-2	9

look like things would get any better as the Aggies went 1-9 in Bryant's first year. But by his third year, the Aggies were Southwest Conference champions, with a 14-14 tie against Houston denying a perfect season. He coached just one more year before leaving for Alabama, where he won six national championships and retired as college football's all-time winningest coach.

R.C. Slocum

(1989-2002, 123-47-2)

The all-time wins leader at A&M, Slocum won 123 games in 14 years, including 73 percent of conference games. He had five seasons of 10 wins or more, won three consecutive Southwest Conference titles and coached the Aggies to the 1998 Big 12 championship with an upset victory over Kansas State.

Year	Record	SWC/Big 12 record	Final ranking
1989	8-4	6-2	20
1990	9-3-1	5-2-1	13
1991	10-2	8-0	12
1992	12-1	7-0	7
1993	10-2	7-0	8
1994	10-0-1	6-0-1	8
1995	9-3	5-2	15
1996*	6-6	4-4	
1997	9-4	6-2	20
1998	11-3	7-1	11
1999	8-4	5-3	23
2000	7-5	5-3	
2001	8-4	4-4	
2002	6-6	3-5	

*First year of Big 12

Dana X. Bible

(1917, 1919-28, 72-19-9)

Bible, the first coach to have any lasting success at A&M, pushed his teams to undefeated seasons in 1917 (8-0), 1919 (10-0) and 1927 (8-0-1). Bible, who also coached basketball and baseball at A&M, went on to be the head coach at the University of Texas. He might have won

Year	Record	Record
1917	8-0	2-0
1919	10-0	4-0
1920	6-1-1	5-1
1921	6-1-2	3-0-2
1922	5-4	2-2
1923	5-3-1	0-3-1
1924	7-2-1	2-2-1
1925	7-1-1	4-1
1926	5-3-1	1-3-1
1927	8-0-1	4-0-1
1928	5-4-1	1-3-1

even more games, but he missed the 1918 season because he was a pilot in World War I.

Homer Norton

(1934-47, 82-53-9)

While some will complain that the Aggies weren't true champions in 1919 or 1927, there's no denying the 1939 team its national title. Norton coached at A&M for 14 years, and his 82 wins rank second. The Aggies won just five games in Norton's first two seasons but went on to win two Southwest Conference titles and shared in another in 1940.

Year	Record	SWC record	Final ranking
1934	2-7-2	1-4-1	
1935	3-7	1-5	
1936	8-3-1	3-2-1	
1937	5-2-2	2-2-2	
1938	4-4-1	2-3-1	
1939	11-0	6-0	1
1940	9-1	5-1	6
1941	9-2	5-1	9
1942	4-5-1	2-3-1	
1943	7-2-1	4-1	
1944	7-4	2-3	
1945	6-4	3-3	
1946	4-6	3-3	
1947	3-6-1	1-4-1	

Horton's team was 29-3 from 1939-41.

Legendary games

Manziel shines as Aggies roll Tide

Behind Johnny Manziel's Heisman-signature performance, the Aggies jumped to a 20-0 first-quarter lead in Tuscaloosa. Alabama's late rally ended when Deshazor Everett intercepted an A.J. McCarron pass at the A&M goal line to help seal the win. Manziel finished with 253 passing yards and two touchdowns, cementing his status as a Heisman front-runner. "No moment is too big for him," coach Kevin Sumlin said. It is the only time the Aggies have beaten a No. 1 team on the road.

AGGIES 29, ALABAMA 24
Nov. 12, 2012

McNeal rallies A&M past No. 1 OU

I n R.C. Slocum's final year as head coach, the Aggies delivered the school's first win over a No. 1 team, with Kevin Sumlin calling the plays at Kyle Field. It was an improbable one, too, as the Aggies benched quarterback Dustin Long and Reggie McNeal came on and threw four touchdown passes. The Aggies and Sooners combined for more than 800 yards, with McNeal accounting for more than 270. "We knew we had Sumlin, he was calling plays, our offense had started rolling," McNeal told Aggiesports.com. "We knew OU was vulnerable. Going into the week, coach said we were going to take shots on them. We knew they were susceptible to that. We felt as a team we could win the game."

AGGIES 30, OKLAHOMA 26

Nov. 9, 2002

A&M dashes title dreams, wins Big 12

I n St. Louis, the Aggies won their first and only Big 12 championship by beating a Kansas State team that was one win from playing

**AGGIES 36,
KANSAS STATE 33**
Dec. 5, 1998

for the national title. Kansas State led 27-12 going into the fourth quarter, but the Aggies rallied behind quarterback Branndon Stewart, who threw a pair of touchdown passes and a two-point conversion to send the game into overtime. In double overtime, running back Sirr Parker took a short pass from Stewart and scampered 33 yards for the win.

Sugar Bowl win caps perfect season

The only Associated Press national title for the Aggies didn't come easy. Despite being the No. 1 team in the country, the Aggies had to play against Tulane in New Orleans. The Aggies trailed the fifth-ranked Green Wave 13-7 in the fourth quarter before John Kimbrough scored his second touchdown on an 18-yard lateral. Kimbrough finished with 159 yards, but it was quarterback Cotton Price's extra point following the second Kimbrough touchdown that proved to be the difference. Kimbrough was second in the Heisman voting the next year, but his coach Homer Norton had no doubt about how good he was in the Sugar Bowl. "He's the greatest football player in the world," Norton said after the game, according to *Sugar Bowl Classic: A History*. "And you can put my name on that with a picture."

Victory starts streak over Longhorns

There wasn't anything particularly exciting about this game. It was just an old-fashioned beating of the then 12th-ranked Longhorns. But what made the game in Austin special was

AGGIES 37
TEXAS 12
Dec. 1, 1984

what it signified. Since 1940, the Aggies had won just seven meetings in their annual matchup against their rivals. But the 1984 game, in which the Aggies were coached by Jackie Sherrill, turned the tide in the series. A&M would reel off six straight wins over Texas and win 10 of 11 in one stretch. The 1984 game itself was a dominant performance, with A&M jumping to a 23-0 lead.

Bonfire game brings sense of relief

Forget that the 24th-ranked Aggies beat the No. 7 Longhorns. The game will always be remembered for being played in the wake of the bonfire tragedy. A&M missed practice time during the week as football players helped in the accident area. Texas had a 16-6 lead at halftime but the Aggies outscored them 14-0 in the second half, with Matt Bumgarner's 14-yard catch from Randy McCown giving the Aggies the lead for good. The game wasn't sewn up until Brian Gamble recovered a late fumble. It certainly was more than just a win over Texas. "The victory and celebration brought a sense of relief for Aggies everywhere — if only for a moment," Bumgarner wrote in *What It Means to Be an Aggie*.

AGGIES 20
TEXAS 16
Nov. 26, 1999

Shutout recorded on Bevo's hide

AGGIES 13
TEXAS 0
Nov. 19, 1915

This was the first game played between the two schools in College Station. Before 1915, the games were either in Austin, Dallas, Houston or San Antonio. The particulars aren't important but the score is: 13-0. That's what the Aggies ended up branding on the Texas mascot in 1917. That escapade gave birth to the legend of Texas' changing the brand to the word *Bevo*. As for the game itself, the 13-0 victory marked the fourth win for the Aggies in a five-game span. Four of the five wins came by shutout.

Heisman winner sacked at Kyle Field

A ndre Ware won the Heisman Trophy in 1989, but he was lucky to escape from College Station with his head in his helmet. The Cougars came into the game ranked eighth and were undefeated behind their run-and-shoot offense under coach Jack Pardee. But the Wrecking Crew dashed Houston's chances at an undefeated season. Ware, who had been sacked nine times all season before the game, was sacked six times and threw for just 247 yards and a touchdown. The highlight was provided by linebacker Aaron Wallace, who sacked Ware hard enough that his helmet flew off. Wallace picked up the helmet and then dropped it on the Kyle Field turf.

AGGIES 17
HOUSTON 13
Oct. 14, 1989

All-time NFL team

QB Gary Kubiak (1980-82) The quarterback pickings are slim out of A&M, but Kubiak proved to be a serviceable backup to John Elway in Denver. Kubiak, an eighth-round pick in 1983, started five games in his nine-year career and ended up throwing 14 touchdown passes.

RB Curtis Dickey (1976-79) While the

Cushing Memorial Library and Archives, Texas A&M University
Curtis Dickey was a first-round pick in 1980.

Aggies have had great seasons by running backs in college, it hasn't always translated in the NFL. Dickey was a first-round pick by the Baltimore Colts in 1980 and played seven years in the NFL, rushing for 4,019 yards. In 1983, he rushed for 1,122 yards and finished ninth in the NFL in all-purpose yards.

RB John David Crow (1955-57) The Heisman winner followed up his stellar Aggie career by being a first-round pick of the Chicago Cardinals in 1958. Crow was a four-time Pro Bowl pick and finished in the top 10 in rushing four times. He ended his career with more than 8,500 combined yards rushing and receiving.

TE Dan Campbell (1995-98) A third-round pick in 1999, Campbell was a blocking first tight end who ended up playing 10 years in the NFL for three teams. Campbell's best season was in 2006, when he caught 21 passes and scored four touchdowns for the Detroit Lions.

OL Richmond Webb (1986-89) Webb, the ninth pick in the 1990 draft by Miami, was one of the most dominant tackles of the 1990s. He was a seven-time Pro Bowl selection and was a two time All-Pro pick.

OL Jerry Fontenot (1985-88) Fontenot was a third-round pick in 1989 played 16 seasons in the NFL. While he never made the Pro Bowl,

Fontenot started 195 games for the Chicago Bears and New Orleans Saints.

OL Steve McKinney (1994-97) McKinney was snapped up by the Indianapolis Colts in the fourth round of the 1998 draft. He started for almost a decade at guard and center for the Colts and the Houston Texans. McKinney finished his career with 133 starts.

OL Geoff Hangartner (2002-04) Hangartner started 12 games in 2012 for the Carolina Panthers. A fifth-round pick in 2005 by Carolina, Hangartner started 15 games his second year and has started 83 of the 108 games he's played in the NFL, bouncing between center and guard.

OL Cody Risien (1976-78) A seventh-round pick in 1979, Risien was a two-time Pro Bowler and played 10 seasons in Cleveland, starting 140 times with the majority of those coming at right tackle.

WR Gerald Carter (1978-79) Solid for some bad Tampa Bay Buccaneer teams, Carter had more than 3,400 receiving yards and scored 17 touchdowns. Not bad for a ninth-round pick.

WR Albert Connell (1995-96) A fourth-round pick in the 1997 draft, Connell played five years in the NFL, with his most productive seasons coming with the Washington Redskins. His big year came in 1999, when he had 1,132 yards and seven touchdowns. He was a big-play threat, averaging 17.8 yards a reception for his career.

Cushing Memorial Library and Archives, Texas A&M University

Tony Franklin was known for his barefoot kicking style.

K Tony Franklin (1975-76) The Philadelphia Eagles used their third-round pick in 1979 on Franklin, and he didn't disappoint. Franklin was regularly in the top 10 in points scored and field-goal percentage. He went to the Pro Bowl in 1986 with New England.

DL Ray Childress (1981-84)

An All-American at Texas A&M, Childress was the Houston Oilers' first pick in 1985. Childress played 12 years in the NFL, and made the Pro Bowl five times with the Oilers. He had 76.5 career sacks, with 13 coming in 1992.

DL Jacob Green (1977-79)

A first-round pick for Seattle in 1980, Green was an anchor for the Seahawks' defensive line for the next decade. He reached double figures in sacks five times and made two Pro Bowls. He ended his career with 97.5 sacks.

DL Sam Adams (1991-93)

A defensive end at A&M, Adams made his career as a force in the middle on the defensive line for six teams. He was a first-round pick by the Seattle Seahawks and earned three trips to the Pro Bowl and ended up playing 14 years.

DL Charlie Krueger (1955-57)

An All-America offensive tackle at A&M, Krueger excelled on the defensive line after being a first-round pick of San Francisco in 1958. He played all 15 of his pro seasons with San Francisco and was a two-time Pro Bowler.

LB Von Miller (2007-10) The two-time All-American was the Associated Press Rookie of the Year in 2011 and has been to the Pro Bowl twice. He's already registered 30 sacks for the Denver Broncos.

LB Jack Pardee (1954-56) One of the Junction Boys, Pardee was a second-round pick by the Los Angeles Rams in 1957. Pardee played 15 years in the NFL, the majority of them with the Rams. He was named an Associated Press first team All-Pro twice.

LB Dat Nyugen (1995-98) He didn't receive the same kind of accolades he did at A&M, where he won the Butkus Award, but Nguyen played seven seasons for the Dallas Cowboys after being a third-round pick in 1996. He started 65 games for the Cowboys but had his career shortened by a neck injury.

Lester Hayes made five trips to the Pro Bowl.

DB Lester Hayes (1973-76) Before he was known for using Stickum for the Oakland Raiders, Hayes was an All-American free safety for the Aggies. Oakland used its fifth-round pick on Hayes in 1977, and he rewarded them with 39 interceptions and five trips to the Pro Bowl.

DB Pat Thomas (1972-75) While Thomas didn't have a lengthy career, he made a strong impression in his seven seasons with the Los Angeles Rams from 1976-82. Thomas went to the Pro Bowl twice and had 26 interceptions.

DB Yale Lary (1949-51) A third-round pick of the Detroit Lions in 1952, Lary was a nine-time Pro Bowler and five-time all-NFL pick for the Lions. He could do it all. In addition to playing safety, he handled the punting chores and did return work for the Lions. He finished with 50 interceptions.

AGGIE FACT

Yale Lary was inducted into the Hall of Fame in 1979.

Yale Lary, who starred at Texas A&M from 1949-51, has the honor of being the only Aggie in the Pro Football Hall of Fame. Lary turned a third-round pick by Detroit into an 11-year career in the NFL. He played safety and punter and returned punts. He had 50 career interceptions and averaged 44.3 yards per punt. He led the NFL in punting average three times and finished in the top 10 in interceptions four seasons. He was inducted in the Class of 1979.

DB Aaron Glenn (1992-93) Picked in the first round of the 1994 draft by the New York Jets, he had 41 interceptions and made three Pro Bowls in a 15-year career.

P Shane Lechler (1996-99) A member of the 10th anniversary all Big 12 team, Lechler signed with the Houston Texans after the 2012 season but went to seven Pro Bowls with Oakland and has averaged 47.5 yards per punt for his career. That's the second-best average of all time.

Cushing Memorial Library and Archives, Texas A&M University

The Aggies lost at Arkansas, 33-21, in 1951 and finished the season 5-3-2.

Index

About the author

Anthony Andro didn't start out as a fan of Texas A&M.

The first time he went to an A&M football game he wasn't even rooting for the Aggies. He

Max Faulkner

came away happy from the 1987 Cotton Bowl because Ohio State won and he got to sit close to the Buckeye cheerleaders.

But a year later Andro was at Texas A&M and on his way to a major in journalism.

After graduating from A&M in 1992, Andro went to work as a sports reporter for the *Port Arthur News*. He moved to Fort Worth in 1999 and worked for the *Fort Worth Star-Telegram* until the summer of 2011, when he moved to Fox Sports Southwest. He's now works in the communications department for the Arlington school district.

Andro lives in Arlington with his Longhorn wife, Diana, and their son, Patrick.